# HOW I GET TO SCHOOL

AUTHOR: Paulle Caccamise

# Dedication Page

The following story is for my beloved nephew, Giovanni Caccamise.

(Read With Rhy-thm On A Pulse)
(Line Space = Natural Musical Rest)

Amidst the morning gray...

... of May,

I travel thirteen miles.

Up-hill... of course... both ways

as-I-carry all my files,

back and forth to school - each day!

13 MILES

. . .Through the ic-y blow of snow

I heave-ho, - heave-ho... can't be slow...

to catch that moving bus

and double transfer to a train.

Then gall-op on Gus, Gus, Gus...

and hop a-board a plane.

Then I bribe to board a ding-y boat

to sail along a moat,

Uggh

of COURSE!

it doesn't stay afloat!

So I surf up on a bill-y goat.

At the river's rocky moss
I pig-gy back an Albatros.
She blasts - off !

My coif goes a loft !

We rise and I'm spring - tossed,
As we nar-row-ly floss through
the nar-row-est crev-asse.

Ex-act-ly half past eight,

I can't be ear-ly - neith-er late

Leap!
Flair!
Shoot!

I ripped my par-a-chute.
So, my land-ing is uncouth.

I cash in a fav-or
with some salt-y chees-y bait.

To be dragged and towed
by my shift-y mous-y 'mate.

Shhh!

Don't Tell

He's got these nift-y rock-et skates.

Rac-ing up 6th A-ve-nue,
I near-ly want to spew.

So I quick-ly flaunt my water shoes,
and paddle my canoe.

The riv-er rush-es, bobs and weaves,

whi-le I bat-tle for-ty thieves.

But all these thieves
are real-ly peeved!...

... In-clud-ing STEVE...

Well,
since the air is thick and mug-gy,
dank and bug-gy

And none can roll up their sleeves...

... All for-ty leave.

Ram-bling down the harbor,

I notice I am drag-gin'

But I see my lit-tle neigh-bor,
with a ti-ny lit-tle wa-gon.

Ac-comp-an-ied by ted-dy bears,

doll pairs

and tea wares.

We gos-sip ov-er col-ored hair and neigh-bor-ly af-fairs...

Thump!

Whump!

Tum-ble and fum-ble...

Ev-ery-thing's a jum-ble.

And all my new friends are in a clut-tered crum-ple.

My <u>cour</u>-i-<u>er</u> has <u>hit</u>

<u>quite</u> the <u>case</u> of <u>stairs.</u>

Which <u>gives</u> <u>my</u> <u>back</u>,

<u>quite</u> the <u>case</u> of <u>scares.</u>

So much time has passed!

And I'm get-ting no-where fast,

If I'm late my time in school won't last...

... and Fa-ther Time will think me daft.

So I give my wa-gon friend a tip...

...and sneak aboard Pi-rate Ship.

Pro-pelled by three e-nor-mous masts

we sail three o-ceans that are vast.

As the whip-ping o-cean waves are crack-ing,

we end up fen-ding off a Kra-ken

with a might-y can-non whack-ing!

So much time has passed!

If I'm late my dreams are dashed.

All me mates will have a laugh,

As fa-ther time thinks me daft.

But, fel-low Pi-rate Gar-y

en-cour-a-ges an out!

A last chance, for a last dance,

yet there's still a hint of doubt

Gary Grum-bles,

"Thar can-non's beens on-ly test-ed on some trout."

I shot up high and be-yond

O-ver fields and ponds,

Break-ing dist-ance through the dunes,

My tar-get's one hot air bal-loon.

through the clouds of heav-y light-ning rain.

I smack into the bas-ket

with surp-ris-ing lit-tle pain.

Soil-ed from the can-non soot:

all in-ev-it-a-ble stains....

I slink down a rope to a cit-y wa-ter drain.

My tail-ored suit:

soaked.

Oh!

What a poor sor-ry bloke.

But!

I'm back on track... and I'm feel-ing pret-ty stoked.

Swim-ming dog-gy pad-dle
with my fi-les on my back,

I washed up to school
and hit the door with a whack!

ELMWOOD
ELEMENTARY

My class is on the 4th floor...

Ad-vance down a hall to the 5th door.

SCIENCE

Here's my chance the Tea-cher's mid snore.

I a-void her glance...

On-ly six desks more!

I wig-gle up the last chair

Of course, all the class stares.

ZZZZ

Quick-ly, raise my hand like I've been there,

Tea-cher gives a smi-le!?...

...NOT A GLARE!?

No <u>need</u> <u>to</u> de-<u>spair</u>

I'm right on time

of course,

with-<u>out</u> a <u>snare</u>!

{The End}

Milton Keynes UK
Ingram Content Group UK Ltd.
UKHW050110201124
451264UK00002B/27